PET PARROTS

Katie John

Grolier
an imprint of

◣SCHOLASTIC

www.scholastic.com/librarypublishing

Published 2009 by Grolier
An imprint of Scholastic Library Publishing
Old Sherman Turnpike
Danbury, Connecticut 06816

For The Brown Reference Group plc
Project Editor: Jolyon Goddard
Editor: Ann Baggaley
Picture Researchers: Clare Newman, Sophie
Mortimer
Designer: Sarah Williams
Managing Editor: Tim Harris

Volume ISBN-13: 978-0-7172-8049-0
Volume ISBN-10: 0-7172-8049-7

**Library of Congress
Cataloging-in-Publication Data**

Nature's children. Set 5.
  p. cm.
  Includes index.
  ISBN-13: 978-0-7172-8084-1
  ISBN-10: 0-7172-8084-5 (set)
  1. Animals--Encyclopedias, Juvenile. I.
Grolier Educational (Firm)
  QL49.N386 2009
  590.3--dc22
                    2008014674

Printed and bound in China

PICTURE CREDITS

Front cover

Back cover

Contents

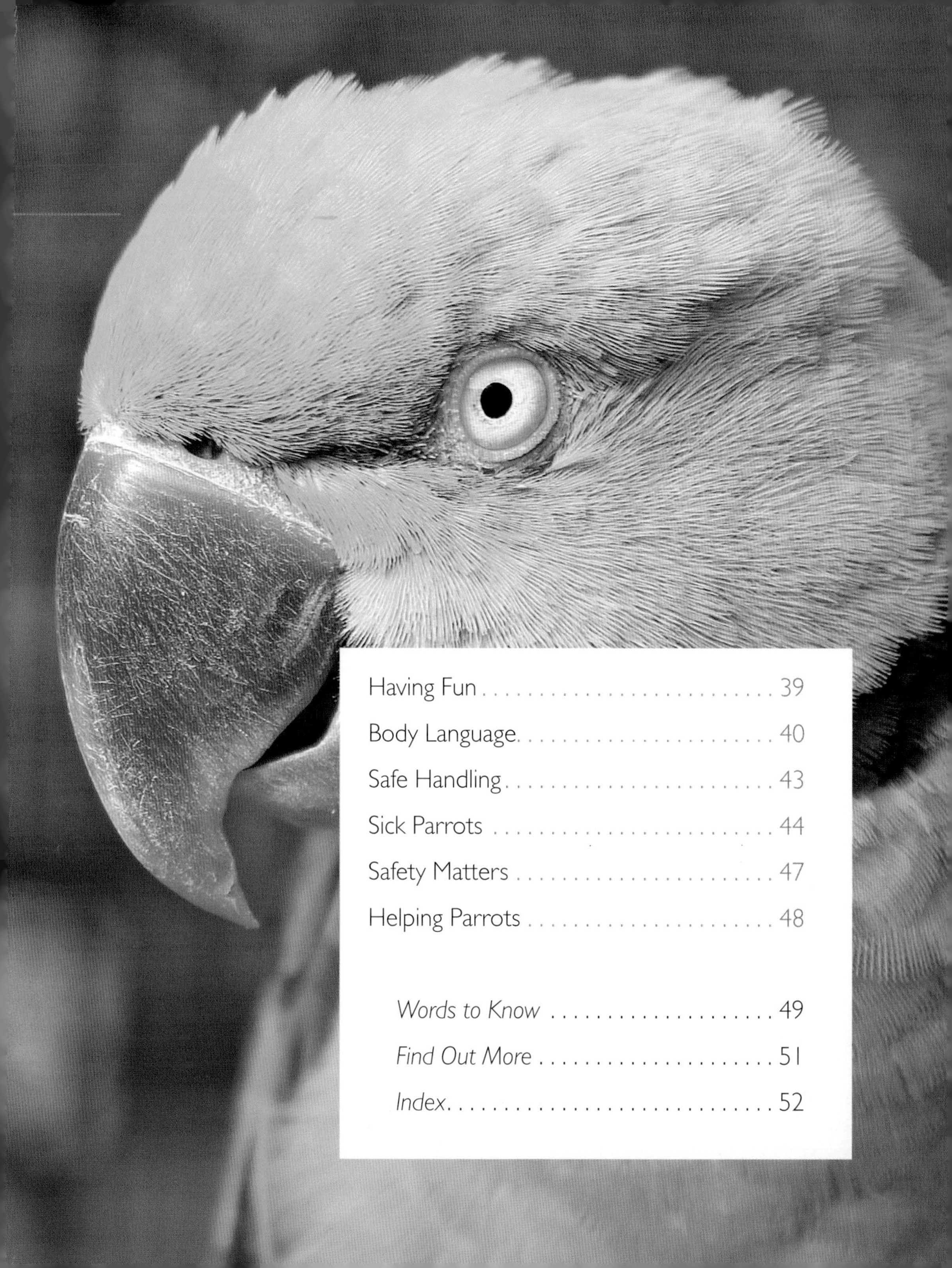

FACT FILE: Pet Parrots

Class	Birds (Aves)
Order	Parrotlike birds (Psittaciformes)
Families	Parrots, macaws, and lories (Psittacidae) and cockatoos (Cacatuidae)
Genera	Various, including lovebirds (*Agapornis*), Amazon parrots (*Amazona*), and macaws (*Ara* and *Anodorhynchus*)
Species	Many; common pet parrots include the ringneck parakeet (*Psittacula krameri*) and the African gray (*Psittacus erithacus*)
World distribution	Found naturally in tropical and semitropical regions, but kept in captivity all over the world
Habitat	Tropical forests and scrublands
Distinctive physical characteristics	Many species have attractive plumage; some, such as macaws, have especially colorful feathers
Habits	Intelligent and "talkative," parrots often get along well with humans, although they need a lot of attention
Diet	Mostly seeds, nuts, and fruit

Introduction

Beautiful and intelligent, parrots have fascinated humans for thousands of years. Some peoples have even seen them as sacred beings. The ancient Muisca people of South America worshiped a parrot god. Hindus see the parrot as a symbol of love. Many people admire these birds because of their colorful **plumage**, or because they can learn tricks and even words.

It is important to remember that all parrots, even those bred in **captivity**, are wild creatures. They are not like dogs, cats, or farm animals, which have been bred by humans for thousands of years. Parrots can be wonderful companions. However, their owners must take time to learn about their natural habits—what they like to eat, where they usually live, and how they communicate.

As pets, parrots are friendly, fun, and sometimes hard work!

Rainbow lorikeets are common in Indonesia and Australia. They sometimes flock in hundreds to feed in the treetops.

Parrots in Nature

In the wild, most parrots live in jungles or rain forests, in regions such as South America, western Africa, and Southeast Asia. Those are warm, bright places, thickly crowded with trees, bushes, fruit, and flowers. There are also thousands of kinds of animals, from noisy monkeys to brilliant butterflies.

Parrots fit in perfectly with their bright, noisy, tree-filled surroundings. They are strong, fast fliers, skilled at swooping through the treetops. Their clever minds enable them to cope with this busy, but sometimes confusing, environment. Their loud voices help them keep in touch with one another in the densest jungle. Even the parrots' messy eating habits, and the way they spray their **droppings** everywhere, help the forest by spreading seeds and **fertilizing** the soil.

Some Australian and South American parrots live in warm, dry woodlands. In a few cases, parrots have even escaped from zoos or homes and become **feral**, taking up residence in cities and parks.

Basic Features

All parrots have certain features in common. They have a hooked beak, tough enough to crack open hard nuts and seeds. They can also use their beak to hold onto things as they climb. A parrot's feet have two toes pointing forward and two pointing backward. That arrangement of toes allows the bird to move around easily in the trees and to grasp pieces of food. Parrots all have narrow, pointed wings. That enables the birds to fly fast and maneuver skillfully in the air. In addition, many types, or **species**, have brightly colored feathers. That plumage makes them highly noticeable in a zoo or home, but in nature it has the opposite effect. The bright feathers help parrots blend in with all the colors of the flowers, fruit, and leaves. That gives them protection by making it more difficult for **predators** to find them.

Parrots use their feet like hands. They tightly grasp food and hold it to their beak while they eat.

Pet parrots of different species often become friends. Here, for example, a scarlet macaw and a blue-and-yellow macaw play a game together.

Social Life

Most kinds of parrots naturally live in **flocks**.
Being with the flock is very important to a parrot.
The other parrots provide company and fun.
More importantly, the birds can keep one
another safe from predators such as monkeys,
snakes, eagles, or even humans.

In some cases, different species flock
together, such as sulfur-crested cockatoos with
rose-breasted cockatoos, or macaws with Amazon
parrots and conures (KON-YURZ). In captivity,
these birds are often happy living with different
bird species.

Other species of parrots, such as African
grays, stay only with their own kind. In captivity,
they might take longer to get used to living with
other birds or animals. They might also protect
their **territory** with more determination.

When parrots live with people, they come
to accept their owner or **handler** as part of the
"flock." A parrot that is well cared for soon
recognizes its owner as a supplier of tasty food
and friendly company.

Noisy Neighbors

All parrot species make noise—but some make more noise than others! Many parrots call, scream, and squawk to one another all day long. They shriek when they wake up in the morning, to greet the rest of their flock. At sunset, the birds shriek to one another again. That way, they know that everybody is present before the flock settles down to **roost** for the night. Parrots screech when they are flying, to keep in touch and to make sure nobody gets lost. They might have special calls to attract a **mate**. If a parrot sees a predator, it might give a loud scream of alarm to warn other parrots nearby. Sometimes parrots squawk just because they are excited.

Pet parrots often talk to their owners in the same way they would to any other members of the flock. An ear-splitting scream might just be a parrot saying, "Good morning!", "Look out—there's a dog!", or "Please don't leave me alone!"

Parrots such as this macaw often learn to "talk" by copying human speech.

Lovebirds breed well in captivity, especially if they are kept in small groups of four or five pairs.

Two's Company

Parrots take between one and four years to become adults. Only then can they produce young, called **chicks**. The larger species take the longest to grow up fully. Once parrots are adults, they are ready to find a mate.

Most parrots are **monogamous** (MUH-NOH-GUH-MUSS), which means they have the same mate for their whole life. Lovebirds are especially well known for their faithfulness and care for each other—in fact, that is how they got their name.

Pairing up is necessary for producing and bringing up chicks. It is also very important for parrots' happiness and well-being. Birds that have paired up spend a lot of time with each other. They might gently **groom** each other's head or, in some cases, feed each other. They also defend their nest together.

Captive parrots can form similarly close, caring friendships with humans. They might enjoy being with their owner, sitting on his or her hand, and having their head gently scratched.

Family Values

Parrots in the wild usually nest in holes in trees. They lay between two and ten eggs, depending on the species. For the first week or so after the eggs **hatch**, the mother stays with the chicks while the father brings back food. After that, both parents share the feeding and care until the young have **fledged**—which is at about three months old.

Parrots teach their chicks all the skills they need for survival. The parent birds show their young how to find and eat different types of foods, live in the flock, and avoid predators. Other flock members often help. For example, the galah, or rose-breasted cockatoo, uses a **crèche** (CRESH). In a crèche, older birds look after and teach young ones that have just fledged.

Different species grow up at different rates. Parrots that live in busy flocks made up of several species, such as different types of Amazon parrots, often become **independent** at a young age. Birds that live with only their own species spend longer with their family group.

The owner of these
African gray chicks has
made them a cozy nest
inside a storage box.

Scarlet macaws are now endangered in the wild because so many of the birds have been captured.

Choosing a Parrot

There are more than 350 species of parrots, ranging in all colors and sizes. The best-known tame species include macaws, kept for their dazzling plumage. Other popular parrots are the highly intelligent African grays, the sociable cockatoos, and the tiny lovebirds.

If you would like to own a parrot, it is best to choose one of the smaller, easier to handle species, such as a parrotlet, lovebird, or conure. These birds can be as colorful and full of personality as the larger species.

The really big parrots, such as macaws and Amazon parrots, need expert care. They must have a specially designed environment where they can fly free and lead a life that is as close as possible to their natural existence. It is better to enjoy these birds in zoos, bird sanctuaries, or rescue centers. If you would like to get more involved with them, you might be able to help as a volunteer in those places.

A Friend for Life

Parrots need company. If they have to live alone, they may become stressed and unhappy, or even physically ill. Ideally, a parrot should have another parrot as a companion. However, they can also form bonds with other creatures—including people. If you are thinking of keeping a parrot, you have to be prepared to spend a lot of time with your bird, and give him or her plenty of attention.

Owning a parrot is a long-term commitment. Even small species, such as lovebirds and lorikeets, can live for longer than most other types of pets—often from 15 to 20 years. The larger African and Amazon parrots, macaws, and cockatoos can live for 50 or 60 years. In fact, one sulfur-crested cockatoo reached more than 80 years of age. It is possible for a parrot to outlive his or her owner. This is just one more reason why the biggest parrots are not normally recommended as pets.

Sulfur-crested cockatoos are well known for developing close bonds with their owners. However, they often become devoted to just one person, and are aggressive toward anyone else.

This Australian parrot's sleek feathers and alert expression show that the bird is both healthy and happy.

Getting Acquainted

Anyone who wants to buy a parrot needs to do a lot of research first. It is not a good decision to choose a parrot in a pet shop because it looks pretty or, worse, buy a bird from the internet. An ideal way to learn about parrots is to meet with a breeder or go to a rescue center and watch people working with the birds. You might even be allowed to handle the parrots yourself. That will give you some idea of what it might be like to share your life with them.

Look for a healthy parrot, with smooth, glossy feathers and bright eyes. Ask how the parrot was reared. It is best to choose a bird that was reared by its parents but handled by people from an early age. Watch how the bird acts with its handler and with you. A well-treated bird will probably be friendly and curious toward you, and loving with its handler. Such a bird is easier to keep than one that is scared of people.

Spreading Out

Even the smallest parrots need room to move. They need a cage that is big enough to fly in and also has room for perches and toys. The best kind is a rectangular cage that is wider than it is high. The bars should be set closely enough together, so that the bird cannot get its head stuck. They must also be strong enough to resist damage from a parrot's claws and beak. The best cages are made of stainless steel, which is strong and nontoxic—not poisonous—to parrots.

The cage should have several perches. You can make extra perches by adding tree branches of different sizes. Choose nontoxic types of woods, such as maple and apple. Wash and dry the branches before putting them in the cage. Your parrot may also enjoy having a box to hide in for a quick sleep or some private time. Lastly, you might need a small padlock for the cage door—some parrots are very good at escaping!

Ideal Surroundings

The best place for a pet parrot is with you and your family. Put the cage in a room where you spend a lot of time, so the parrot can see everyone and watch what is going on. Choose a place where you can safely let your bird out of the cage to fly about and play.

Your parrot's cage needs to be in a place that gets plenty of sunlight. However, do not put the cage too close to a window where there is likely to be strong sunlight, because your bird might get too hot. Also avoid placing the cage near a door, because your bird might get chilled by drafts. Placing the cage against a wall or in a corner may make your parrot feel more secure.

Parrots are very sensitive to smoke, chemical fumes, and gases. Never put a cage in a place where people use paint, cleaning products, or aerosol sprays. Never keep a cage in a kitchen, because fumes from cooking can kill a bird.

African grays make great companions, but they need plenty of entertainment and attention. If they are bored or stressed they may develop behavioral problems, like biting.

Essential Chores

Keeping your parrot's cage clean might not be your favorite task, but it is vital for the bird's health. The bottom of the cage needs to be lined, to catch droppings and spilled food. Newspaper is ideal. However, do not use pages with colored pictures on them. The ink may be harmful to your bird. The lining should be changed daily.

Every week, wash the floor of the cage, and the perches, with hot water and a little soap. First, take your parrot out of the cage and put him or her in a safe place. Ask someone else to look after the bird while you work. Scrub the cage floor and perches with a brush, then rinse everything thoroughly to get these areas really clean. Make sure the cage is completely dry before you put your bird back in.

Once a month, wash the whole cage, including the wires, with very hot water and a nontoxic detergent, to kill germs.

This type of cage is suitable only for small parrots, such as lovebirds. It can be wheeled around to keep the birds out of drafts and direct sunlight.

These conures are enjoying a bowl of sunflower seeds. Parrots are messy eaters, and usually scatter seed husks around for their owners to sweep up!

What a Mess!

No matter how clean you keep your parrot's home, the bird will not do the same for you! Parrots make a lot of mess, and there is nothing you can do to stop them. The area around their cage is likely to get dirty—and when you let your parrot out, the mess just spreads.

Parrots leave droppings everywhere they go. They also spill food and throw around waste such as seed **husks**. They naturally shed a few feathers. And when they **preen** themselves, they also shed dust and flakes of skin.

You can help keep things clean by covering any furniture or surfaces that you don't want to get dirty. Scrape up droppings, and sponge soiled areas with warm water and soap. You might have to accept that a little mess is just part of having a parrot.

Healthy Eating

In the wild, parrots eat a mixture of fruit, nuts, and seeds. They might also eat small amounts of soil or clay, which supply them with **minerals**. Your parrot will need a similarly mixed diet.

Pet stores sell special parrot foods. Check which type is suitable for your bird. Your parrot will also need fresh food, chopped up so that it is easy to eat. Parrots enjoy fruits—such as bananas, apples, grapes, oranges, and berries—and a variety of vegetables. Carrots, lettuce, corn, and dark, leafy vegetables such as spinach are healthy choices. Never give your parrot avocado—it is toxic to birds. You can also offer nuts, as long as they are unsalted. To lessen the risk of toxic chemicals, you should choose the type of nuts that are sold for people to eat.

Feed your parrot twice a day, and clean the food bowl between meals, so germs do not collect there. The bird also needs freshwater at all times. It is best to use a water bottle, and change the water every day.

A parrot's strong, curved beak has a sharp point. It is ideal for breaking open the tough shells of nuts.

An eclectus parrot shakes out its wings to dry them after a bath. Natural oils prevent the feathers from becoming waterlogged.

34

Good Grooming

Like most birds, parrots clean their feathers by preening. That is a very important job, as it keeps the feathers in good condition.

Preening cleans and straightens the feathers, and dislodges loose ones when the bird is **molting**. The parrot rubs its beak on a "preen gland," at the base of its tail, which produces oil. It then strokes the oil over its feathers to keep them supple and waterproof. The parrot may also nibble the edges of the feathers. That "zips them up" so that the strands of each feather are smoothly joined together. However, there are some places that parrots cannot reach, such as their head or the back of their neck. That is when they need another parrot—or a person—to groom these spots for them.

Parrots also enjoy bathing, or being gently sprayed with a shower or plant spray. A bath followed by a good preening session is ideal for keeping feathers at their best.

Things to Chew

A parrot's beak is an essential tool for feeding, climbing, grooming, and playing. The outer covering of the beak is made of keratin, the same substance as fingernails. Like fingernails, the beak grows constantly. It has to be "filed down" so that it stays sharp and in good condition. In the wild, this happens naturally as a parrot uses its beak to peel fruit, crack nuts, climb branches, and dig into bark. Captive parrots chew their perches or tree branches in their cage. You can buy special parrot chew toys made from wood or strong acrylic. Pieces of coconut shell, with the tasty coconut still inside, are good for chewing, too. Another idea is to give your parrot the rawhide "bones" that are made for dogs to chew.

Big parrots such as macaws can damage their cage by chewing, unless the bars are extra strong.

Parrots enjoy playing with toys that they can pick up or throw around. You should make sure there are no small parts that your parrot could swallow.

Having Fun

Because they are highly intelligent birds, parrots need plenty of things to keep them occupied. They love playing with one another and with people. But if they have to spend time alone, toys help keep them amused. It is a good idea to have a selection of toys. Just offer your parrot two or three at a time. That stops the bird from becoming bored with them.

You can buy parrot toys of all kinds that are made from nontoxic materials. Choose toys that are a comfortable size for your bird to handle easily with its beak and feet. A ball or ring makes an ideal toy.

Homemade toys can provide amusement, too. A strong, knotted rope made from hemp can be fun—your bird may spend hours trying to undo it! Toilet roll centers are satisfying to rip up. You could also give food that has to be opened before eating, such as corncobs still in their husks and nuts in their shells.

Body Language

Parrots communicate by actions as well as noises. They often use this "body language" to show their feelings.

A happy parrot may fluff out its feathers gently, wag its tail like a dog, or perhaps pull up one of its legs. The bird may also grind its beak quietly. Another sign of happiness is when a parrot slowly stretches out the wing and leg on one side, and then the other—almost like someone doing yoga!

If a parrot feels nervous, it may ruffle its feathers or pull them tight against its body, and its wings will quiver. A parrot that is angry may ruffle its feathers and fan out its tail. Angry birds sometimes crouch down and sway from side to side. They may growl, hiss, or snap with their beak. If that kind of warning is ignored, a parrot will probably bite, although biting is usually only a last resort.

Raised feathers are a natural reaction to any disturbing event. This parrot is expressing alarm and anger.

A parrot that has learned to trust people will happily accept handling. This small parrot is not biting its owner but giving him a nibble to express friendship.

Safe Handling

It is important to get your bird used to being held and carried. The main rules are to be calm, kind, and consistent. Give plenty of praise and perhaps a treat when your bird does what you want. Ignore any unwanted behavior. Never punish parrots—they cannot understand and you will just frighten them.

The first skill to teach your parrot is stepping on or off your hand when asked. To teach stepping on, hold your hand upright with your index finger under the bird's stomach, and say "UP" or "STEP UP." Praise your parrot when it does the right thing. For getting down, hold your bird slightly below a perch, and say "OFF" or "DOWN." Choose one word for each action, and use it every time. For your safety, do not let your bird sit on your shoulder or get close to your face.

Sick Parrots

If your parrot is feeling unwell, you may not notice at first. Parrots naturally conceal signs of weakness, in case predators notice and attack them. It is best to check your parrot every day, so you will quickly see any changes. Your bird's eyes and nose should be clean. The feathers should be smooth and shiny, with no dirtiness around the **vent**. The droppings should be distinct lumps of a greenish and whitish color.

A sick parrot might eat less, and be quieter, than usual. The bird might sit hunched up, perhaps on the bottom of the cage, with its feathers fluffed out and its wings drooping. The droppings may be runny or a different color from normal. You might hear your bird sneezing or breathing noisily. If you see these signs, take your bird to an animal doctor, or veterinarian, as soon as possible.

Giving medicine to a sick bird is a job that only an experienced handler should attempt.

Parrots often get along
well with other family
pets. However, the
animals should never
be left alone together.

Safety Matters

There are various steps you can take to keep your parrot safe and healthy. One of the most important safety measures is to protect parrots from chemicals in the air. Parrots have sensitive lungs that are damaged easily. Never use any kind of aerosol spray—such as fly killer or air freshener—near your bird. Do not burn candles in the room where you keep your parrot. And do not allow people to smoke in the room. Also, make sure there are no houseplants or flowers within reach of your bird. Many plants, including fig trees, amaryllis, tulips, and peonies, are poisonous to parrots.

Before you let your bird out of its cage, check that all doors and windows are shut in your home. Put away anything that your parrot could swallow or break. Stay with the bird at all times. Keep it away from electrical cords, heaters, and ceiling fans. Lastly, check where your parrot is before you walk anywhere or sit down. It is very easy to sit or walk on a bird.

Helping Parrots

Most captive parrots are now specially bred, but sadly some are still taken from the wild. About 3,600 wild parrots are imported into the United States each year. They suffer terrible stress as they are transported around the world and find themselves in a strange place.

Often, parrot trade is both unnecessary and cruel. One way to help end it is to support parrot **conservation** organizations. If you are buying a parrot, make sure it is not a bird that was captured in the wild.

Parrots make rewarding pets but they might also turn out to be more than their owners bargained for. Sadly, it is not uncommon for people to release into the wild a bird that is hard to handle. Parrots need nearly as much time, care, and understanding as children! The more people learn about these wonderful birds, the better protected they will be.

Words to Know

Captivity   When an animal is kept in a zoo, nature park, or someone's home.

Chicks   Young birds.

Conservation   The protection of wild animals, plants, and their habitats.

Crèche   A group of young birds, watched over by older members of the flock.

Droppings   Waste from a bird's body.

Feral   A word used for an animal that has escaped from captivity and gone back to living in the wild.

Fertilizing   Enriching soil with nutrients.

Fledged   When a young bird grows its first full set of feathers.

Flocks   Groups of parrots living together.

Groom   To clean and tidy the feathers of a bird or fur of a mammal.

Handler   A person who looks after or trains animals.

Hatch   To break out of an egg.

Husks	The tough outer coats of seeds.
Independent	Able to live alone without help from parents.
Mate	Either of a breeding pair of animals; to come together to produce young.
Minerals	Substances that make up rocks and soil. Some minerals are also found in plants.
Molting	Losing old feathers as new ones grow to replace them.
Monogamous	Describing animals that mate for life.
Plumage	Another word for feathers.
Predators	Animals that hunt other animals.
Preen	To use the beak to smooth and straighten the feathers.
Roost	To settle down before going to sleep.
Species	The scientific word for animals of the same kind that breed together.
Territory	An area that an animal defends as its own private space.
Vent	An opening in a bird's body, where droppings come out.

Find Out More

Books

Altman, L. J. *Parrots*. Perfect Pets. New York:
Benchmark Books, 2000.

Johnson, J. *Parrot*. Zoo Animals in the Wild. Bel Air,
California: Smart Apple Media, 2006.

Web sites

Bird Care: The 411
www.aspca.org/site/PageServer?pagename=kids_pc_bird_411
Tips on looking after pet birds, including cockatiels.

Cockatoos
www.enchantedlearning.com/subjects/birds/printouts/
Cockatoo.shtml
Facts about cockatoos and a picture to print and color in.

Index